Let's Write-London 2025

Edited by
Naino Masindet and Tom Mallender

Write-London.com

Published in 2025 by Write-London CIC
www.write-london.com

The rights of the author have been asserted under Section 77 of the Copyright, Design and Patents Act 1988 to be identified as the author of their work.

A CIP catalogue record for this title is available from the British Library
ISBN 9798263799281

All rights reserved by the author.
This publication was created in partnership between Write-London and the authors. No part of this publication may be reproduced, stored or transmitted in any form or by any means, graphic, electronic, recorded or mechanical, without the prior written permission of a representative of the author.

Write-London and the production and printing of this book is supported using public funding by Arts Council England via Grants for the Arts and the National Lottery

Let's Write-London 2025

Thanks

Write-London would never succeed without the help and support of all our partners and their generosity. We would like to thank specifically:

Alison, Katy, Riz and the rest of the team at The Wellbeing & Recovery College (West London NHS Trust)

Catherine, Daisy and everyone else at West Central London Mind

Mandy and Amanda of Hammersmith and Fulham Libraries and all the staff at Shepherds Bush Library.

Julie and everyone at Sands End Associated Projects In Action (SEAPIA)

Nina and the whole team at Sands End Arts & Community Centre

SOBUS, Young Hammersmith and Fulham Foundation, The Traveller Movement, Spread the Word, West London Queer Project, It's Not Your Birthday But...

Sharon Tomlin, Benjamin Still, Naino Masindet, Chris Bird, Polly Archer and Yaiza Freire-Bernat

Lastly, and most importantly, we would like to thank each and every participant whose hard work made this book possible.

Introduction

Write-London has a foundational belief that everyone has a story to tell. We exist to help those stories be heard.

Since 2014, Write-London has been facilitating creative workshops in local communities collaborating with people of all ages and abilities to both express themselves and explore their creativity.

Starting in autumn 2024, Let's Write-London worked as a series of over 100 workshops held in partnerships with West Central London Mind, The Wellbeing & Recovery College (West London NHS Trust) & Shepherds Bush Library. Without the co-operation and support of all our partners this project could not have worked so please know you have our sincere thanks.

Most importantly, we would like to say thank you to everyone who has taken part in Let's Write-London. It is all of you that make each and every Write-London project the success that it is.

- Tom Mallender & Naino Masindet

Write-London Directors August 2025

Editor's Note: Every effort has been made to ensure the work published in this volume conforms to the author's original writing. A few slight alterations have had to be made for formatting and space reasons during the typesetting process.

Contents

A Love Letter to Poetry by Kit McDade	- 1
Trees by Marcela Fontes	- 2
Dandelion Seed by Annabella	- 3
Untitled #1 by Diane B	- 4
The Light by Taj Singh Puri	- 5
Losing My Temper by Pam Innes	- 6
Out of the Depths by Arthur Stanfield	- 7
Three Haikus by Taj Singh Puri	- 8
Ode to a Retired Toothbrush by J. H. Frost	- 9
The Quiet Joys of an Afternoon by Kit McDade	- 10
Wanderlust by Pam Innes	- 11
My Story by Leslie Aldridge	- 12
Early Days by Annabella	- 13
PTSD/Stigma by Yaiza Freire-Bernat	- 14
There Is a Bluebird in My Heart That Wants to Get Out by Barbara L	- 15
The Kentucky Mandolin by Taj Singh Puri	- 16
Sand Between Our Toes by Zaneta C	- 17
My First Car by J. H. Frost	- 18
Glasses by Mark Holder	- 19
Happiness by Maria Davis	- 20
Untitled #2 by Diane B	- 21
Therapy by Leslie Aldridge	- 22
Pigeon's Wisdom by Ruth G	- 23
Such Sweet Sorrow by Yaiza Freire-Bernat	- 24
The BFG (Brain Fog Gremlin) by Pam Innes	- 25
The Life of Air by Siân-y-Blewyt	- 26
The 2 Versions of Haggis (To Be Read in	

a Scottish Brogue) by Mark Holder	- 28
2008 by Kaze S	- 29
Charity Shop - A Final Destination by Annabella	- 31
Untitled Haiku by Diane B	- 32
Untitled One by Ruth G	- 33
Proud/افتخار by Arash Niroomand	- 34
Inanimate Objects Sitcom by Kit McDade	- 36
The Ride by Arthur Stanfield	- 37
Cash in Marylebone by Webster Forrest	- 38
Creative Writing by Leslie Aldridge	- 42
Maze of Thoughts by Annabella	- 43
My Body Is by Kit McDade	- 44
An Apartment on 8th Avenue by Mark Holder	- 45
Somewhere Safe by Tom Mallender	- 46
Casos e Acasos/Cases and Coincidences by Marcela Fontes	- 47
Becoming Young by J. H. Frost	- 48
Haiku by Barbara L	- 50
My Last Sunset by Kaze S	- 51
Untitled #3 by Diane B	- 54
Pigeon on the Pond - Gunnersbury Park by Salma A	- 55
Trauma by Leslie Aldridge	- 56
There's a Saying… by Annabella	- 57
From Welcome to Farewell/خوش آمدید سے الوداع تک by Aisha Noor	- 58
Third Date Woes by Kit McDade	- 59
For Decoration Only by Mark Holder	- 60
5pm Rush Hour by Yaiza Freire-Bernat	- 61
Advice by Annabella	- 63

Changing the Bed by Pam Innes	- 64
Untitled Two by Ruth G	- 65
Yesterday's Yearnings by Arthur Stanfield	- 66
John Coltrane by Chris Bird	- 67
The Sounds Around by Taj Singh Puri	- 68
Untitled #4 by Diane B	- 69
The Popping Parade of Popcorns by Aisha Noor	- 70
Haiku 1-3 by Pam Innes	- 74
Time Travel by Maria Davis	- 75
Coming of Age by Kit McDade	- 77
Staring Out Over the Sea by Leslie Aldridge	- 78
The Unexpected Chord by Mark Holder	- 79
About the House by Siân-y-Blewyt	- 80
Rituals–Balance by Annabella	- 81
Ravens by Marcela Fontes	- 82
It Was Red by Taj Singh Puri	- 83
Listen Without Prejudice by Pam Innes	- 85
What Does It Mean That "Out of the Abundance of the Heart the Mouth Speaks" (Luke 6:45)? by Siân-y-Blewyt	- 86
Missed Flight by Salma A	- 87
The Best Room by Barbara L	- 88
Conditional Attraction by Kit McDade	- 89
Dad Is in the Car by Webster Forrest	- 90
Four Haikus by Siân-y-Blewyt	- 92
The Secret Life of a Tree by Marcela Fontes	- 94
Seasons of Change by Maria Davis	- 95
Haiku 4-6 by Pam Innes	- 96
The Soundtrack of Our Home by Siân-y-Blewyt	- 97

Does Anyone Remember Uncle Holly?
by Mark Holder — 98
Co-Conspirators of Hope by Zaneta C — 99
The Idea by Taj Singh Puri — 100
Two Friends Like the Same Person
by Maria Davis — 101
Come on England by Pam Innes — 104
A Familiar Conundrum by Yaiza Freire-Bernat — 106
Spiders by Lauren Storey — 107
Never Judge Books by Covers or Looks
From Lovers by Clare Smith — 108
The Gender Euphoria of Vans by Kit McDade — 110
The Moment by Arthur Stanfield — 111
The Light by the Sea by S. Ahmed — 112
Tit for Tat by Webster Forrest — 113
Untitled #5 by Diane B — 116
Tempo/Time by Marcela Fontes — 117
Life's Journey by Maria Davis — 119
Refraining My Baggage by Kit McDade — 120
Warm Embrace by Yaiza Freire-Bernat — 121
Paparazzi by Zaneta C — 122
Harmonica by Lauren Storey — 123
My Trusty Screwdriver by J. H. Frost — 124
Lionel by Mark Holder — 125
Oh, Milton, Where Art Thou? by Pam Innes — 126
Blossom Haiku/An Ode to Pepperoni Pizza
by Kit McDade — 127
Untitled #6 by Diane B — 128
Woodpecker/داركوب by Arash Niroomand — 129
Fallen by J. H. Frost — 131

Cave by Annabella	- 132
The Shoe by Leslie Aldridge	- 133
Being Still by Marcela Fontes	- 134
Untitled #7 by Diane B	- 135
The Wardrobe of Bess by Lauren Storey	- 136
Everyday Magic by Maria Davis	- 137
Dementia Days by Annabella	- 138
I Left My Heart in Cyprus by Kit McDade	- 139
I Don't Like Being Me by J. H. Frost	- 140
Funeral by Webster Forrest	- 143
Phoenix Star by T M David	- 149
Alum Rock by Aisha Noor	- 158

A Love Letter to Poetry by Kit McDade

Poems are little portals
Each one conjuring new worlds
Or ways of thinking

Succinct little tapas of words
I gobble them up
And write my own

The rhymes make me smile
The evocative imagery
Allow my tears to flow

The form tells a story
All on its own

So pick up your pen
Or open a new Google Doc
And continue the ancient tradition!

Connect to your emotions
And carry on this very human mission!

Trees by Marcela Fontes

Branches interconnected,
Whispering thoughts,
Observing life
In movement and stillness.
Roots absorbing energy,
Sharing thoughts,
Interconnecting.
Roots, intertwined,
Shared thoughts.
Casting shadows,
Breathing.
Living.

Dandelion Seed by Annabella

See all eternity in a dandelion seed
A seasonal reminder of summer lazy days
A dandelion seed
Now separated from its family
Where it grew, independent yet together
Nurtured
Loved so very much
Valued, wanted, yet unconvinced
Now flying where the breeze carries it
Where the wind takes it
Being released time and time again
To new lands, new skies
So light and free

Untitled #1 by Diane B

Taking in the rays
  Feeling the warmth
  Listening to the birds
And to a breeze through the trees
and across your face
drifting
        floating
                resting
                        relaxing

The Light by Taj Singh Puri

I remember the Light.
It was a Saturday morning.
I woke up to a room so bright!

Curtains taken down,
Revealing clear blue skies,
Wow! What a sight!

The scent of fresh spring cotton laundry,
Stripped bedsheets,
All is dazzling white!

My family, spring cleaning since hours before. But me?
Awakening from slumber to a heavenly delight!

A fresh spring breeze
Flowing through open windows and rooms,
The scene never occurred again, try as I might.

I've often wondered: Was it all just a dream?
False memories at night?
But, no! For as surreal as it may have been,
I remember the Light.

Losing My Temper by Pam Innes

Shaking from the ricochets of angry words,
verbal bullets strafing the air
and rebounding resoundingly from the walls,
I swallowed my emotions,
pushing them deep out of sight inside.

Metamorphosis into an invisible child,
unseen as well as unheard.

Over the years, the magma bubbled
and raged below my caldera,
eroding me from within.

Fearing the devastation of eruption,
I diverted the anger into
self-corrosion and excoriation,
becoming outwardly dormant, almost extinct.

Decades later, exhausted, I launch the search
to find my lost temper,
to find healthy ways to relieve the pressure
and begin slowly to heal.

Out of the Depths by Arthur Stanfield

Watching the scrub bank from the moving District line train. The natural focal point of the city dweller. The dreams, the sorrows, the apparent reality.

Years earlier I knew how the now would pan out. That ghostly spiritual sentiment and solid centre of necessary stamina. Nothing is missing, nothing lacks.

The emptiness is all. The truth is out there. It is clarity and does not make promises it cannot keep. The world rotates no matter how we try to stop it.

The taxi, the centre, the bus, the edges. The pavement, that thin tightrope. The quest, the duel.

The show begins to wind down as destinations become close. The sun does its job and for a moment the people rejoice. Me too. Spring has made itself known.

Three Haikus by Taj Singh Puri

Autumn Leaves
Blue skies in autumn,
Purifying air—fresh crunch!
Don't need the warm scarf.

*

Coffee in Mug
Coffee mug sits still.
Milky brown - perfect circle.
Sip. Circle goes down.

*

Jimi
Hippy summer vibes.
Electric guitar strings—squeezed.
Now the drums join!

Ode to a Retired Toothbrush ^{by J. H. Frost}

Oh, how I've exhausted you!
Your bristles once stood proud,
scrubbing mornings out of sleepless nights.

Now dulled, bowed from every angle,
you rest in dusty quiet,
no longer polishing smiles.

A bit cruel, to end like this?
So I take thou
to the corners of the tiger's bowl.
You shall reach where the beast feasts,
and catch what the mischief leaves behind.

Gentler now,
not for mercy,
but for time.
I see you and I smile,
not for what you were,
but for what you still are.

Let us celebrate,
the time of our lives.

The Quiet Joys of an Afternoon _{by Kit McDade}

The afternoon is my favourite time of day
Where the morning has grumbled by
And the evening stretches out before us
Like a red carpet unfurling
I lay back in my sun lounger
Clouds softly swirling overhead
One cloud is a duck, another a cactus
The warm sun blankets the garden
In a saffron hue
Birds sing sweetly overhead
Signalling that all is safe
I sink into the chair
Letting the soft mesh hold my weight
And all my woes
My cat Mona sleeps underneath,
Making use of the shade I provide
The wind permeates jasmine through the air
Nature's perfume
A sweet Solorio coats my tongue
Each languid lick a meditative joy
To-do lists can wait
The only thing to do here is live

Wanderlust by Pam Innes

A path untravelled and uncertain
Through somewhere beyond imagination.
Calf-burning hills and swooping falls
Buffeted and cheered on by squalls and gales

Going deeper and deeper into the unknown
From wild outcrops and brooding moors
To sunshine and bluebirds.

Where is the path?
      Inside of me.
Where does it lead?
      From woe and grief
          To acceptance and peace…

My Story by Leslie Aldridge

My story starts in a children's home
A three-month-old baby who couldn't crawl or roam
As a child without parental support
I was bewildered, scared and wanted to be left alone.

New parents, new home, a total new life.
I would run away to deal with strife.
My life changed joining the Navy
Although my career was not wavy

I progressed in life with energy and smile
To overcome sadness for a while.
Looking back on my life makes me shudder,
but I became a nurse to care for others.

My path in life was to help in health.
To become a nurse was for myself.

Early Days by Annabella

I had such a powerful dream once
I was passing daffodils nodding
I felt happy and safe
But
I became lost
Underneath the earth I found myself
I'd turned to coal
There's no escaping feelings
Too powerful to be ignored
Feelings layered like strata
Pressing earlier feelings into something so hard,
Like coal
Dense, black, dead
… but then I reflect
With the right actions, resources
Coal burns, it glows
It comforts
Keeps me warm
Don't leave the coal in the bucket in the corner, Anna
It's a waste

PTSD/Stigma by Yaiza Freire-Bernat

I wish people understood
what it's like to have your entire past
become your present.
Reliving all situations at once,
your brain exploding.
When I think I've solved it,
it keeps coming back.
I wish people understood
it's not a choice, don't just wake up
and decide to feel sorry for myself.

*

The more we share, the stigma dies,
the world can feel less alone
when we know what each of us have had to survive.

Here's to listening without judgement,
don't pretend to know what someone else
has gone through,
just be humble and kind.

There Is a Bluebird in My Heart That Wants to Get Out by Barbara L

Now I feel confused.
Is it a bluebird
or a yellow bird
or is it a robin?
Plenty of robins live
in my small garden
sitting on the thorny branches of my tree
Singing, eating
raising their young
bathing and splashing
in the bird pool.
There are also blue tits
sharing the tree
with the robins and other birds.
Their names I don't know.
No, there is no
bluebird in my heart.
The birds are here in my garden.

The Kentucky Mandolin by Taj Singh Puri

When hip-hop failed,
I turned to Led.
And there in the background,
I found you instead.

An elvish-stringed tinkle,
My hands wanted a go!
So I bought you in no time,
And you arrived with a glow.

The shiny brown wood,
Black around the edge,
My fingers began plucking,
Your sound soothed my head.

At first it was fun,
You goaded me on.
Then you needed tuning,
And the chores had begun.

Now you sit in the corner,
Dusty and dim,
I don't play with you,
And you've lost your grin.

Oh why did I rob you
Of a home where you'd begin
A true Led Zeppelin musician's story
Of the Kentucky Mandolin?

Sand Between Our Toes by Zaneta C

Clacton-on-Sea, what a way to spend £20!
On a coach, squished against people who don't wanna
become friends with me.

Each prick of stone chiselled by the waves makes me
crave inland, the pier, everything else.
The sea seems all the more unwelcoming, a typical
British grey.

"Oh no," rain pours down,
it's the end of our day.

Umbrellas upend us. Boring relatives suspend our
disbelief with story,

I try to catch the cosplayers dressed as Deadpool,
Superman, even the limited edition cars grace the land.
Clacton-on-Sea, we've all been duped.

Ice cream for five pounds,
we don't give a hoot.

My First Car by J. H. Frost

I
your weight in motion—
a loyal, silent shadow
weathering my storms

II
I don't want to leave
you carry my impatience
and all that I am

III
You lift up my soul
hold my sensitivities
where else would I be

Glasses by Mark Holder

"They were right here a minute ago."

"Here we go, glasses?"

"Yeah."

"You do realise that you've got some on already."

"Yeah, but it's my readers I can't find."

"Lounge?"

"Probably, I'll check—no, not in there. This is mad, where the fuck are they?"

"Well, if they're not in here or the lounge—can only be kitchen, hallway or bathroom."

"Nope, checked everywhere. Perhaps I left them somewhere while I was out."

(Mark picks up a book)

"Hang on, these are my readers."

Happiness by Maria Davis

Happiness, you ask me mine
In the form of the senses that scatter in my mind
I'm not really sure, I say, and it's true
that my senses all rolled into one.
But try and separate them, you ask,
and the scene that makes me smile is gone.
What about smell, I hear you say
And all I can fixate on is the sound
of all that could be rolled into one.
Back to the one.
Ok, what about sound, now that I can relate,
music in 438 and 808,
or whatever the frequency is that happiness comes from
It seems to work as the cats chase my feet.

Untitled #2 by Diane B

An old wooden bookcase
Made of slats and quite wobbly
That my daughter had when small.
Doodles stickers drawings writings on all.

A new place to live
and no shelving for a pantry
I know what I can use

Each piece becomes a shelf
Of a larger project in mind

When I take something out to use
I glimpse the unfaded drawings and doodles.

Therapy by Leslie Aldridge

I remember the war I was in
I try to forget the memories,
putting them in the bin
Through therapy and identifying my trauma
I'm losing them much sooner
By keeping records and writing more
My scrambled memories are not so sore
I'm thankful for this remedy
If any doubts, carry on with therapy.

Pigeon's Wisdom by Ruth G

Patiently I gaze at my surroundings
in search of the love of my life that soon will appear
among our pigeon crowd

She will be perfectly imperfect, be that as it may
We will be till death as part
I know this moment is near
when true love will be fulfilled

Meanwhile I notice this strange humankind
who move around rambling
alone without another soul nearby

Their search for a mate seems so harsh,
in perpetual pursue of a perfect match
they lose all their time, before you know it,
they die without offsprings or
realising we pigeons hold the wisdom
of a good-lived life.

Such Sweet Sorrow by Yaiza Freire-Bernat

His parting is always with such sweet sorrow,
I don't know what to do in the face of tomorrow.
He is my rock and absolute king,
Whenever I feel sad, he makes me glint.

And so, I grab some ink to write how I feel.
It really does make me heal,
I know that if it starts again
I just pick up my pen and write amen.

The BFG (Brain Fog Gremlin) by Pam Innes

He lives in my head.
Most of the time, he's asleep or lying low.

When he comes out to play, he'll replace the word
you want to say with a deafening gap.

When he's feeling really naughty, he'll replace the word
with another random word.

Just for kicks.
The BFG's idea of a joke.

The Life of Air by Siân-y-Blewyt

Air is my favourite element.
So, wind is my sacred sound.

It always has and always will be
my favourite sound unbound.

You can't see it, obviously,
but its effects are all about.

You can actually reach out and touch it,
Well, if it's force 10 gale.

But almost every single day,
its caress will touch your face.

Most often you can hear it,
and is almost never dull.

It's in the rustle of leaves in a tree,
and in the dancing of a chime,

it's that *zhhhhuuuuu* sound in your ear
that goes up and down in tone.

It's in the flapping of a gazebo,
and always in a harbour,
the clang, clang, clang of metal pulleys,
against the tall sail poles.

It's in a whirlwind of dried leaves,
it's the spattering of sheeting rain.

It's the crackle & pop of a fire,
it's in the dancing flame.

There's nothing more I like to listen to
than the sounds in wind's domain.

The 2 Versions of Haggis (To Be Read in a Scottish Brogue) by Mark Holder

One of mae favourite feasts is a haggis
Wae neeps & tatties ain the side
Washed down wae a single malt whiskey
Wae water that flows to the Clyde

Mae Jen thinks I'm awful disgustin'
What wae all the blood ain all the guts
She's happy to eat her veggie one
Made of oats and of grain and of nuts

2008 by Kaze S

After the last customer, she rushes to lock the door, turning over the 'we are open' sign to 'go away.' She closes the door, and now the 5-to-9 is all hers until tomorrow.

But there was the treacherous journey: rush hour on the District Line. Only one thing would outweigh all of this—music. The growing sound between her ears, melting away the fact that she is stuck in the capitalistic 9-to-5.

Without interrupting her tempo, she reaches into her pocket to increase the volume to suffocate the American tourists, the after-work pub goers and the ongoing ambulance. Every footstep is in rhythm and swerves past people like a BMW driver. Her hair flowing back and forth on her back, feeling the wind combing through her knots.

Not even the cars stop her, holding out her hand to say thank you, but in an entitled manner, just like her customers.

Entering the station, the arrival board shows a train approaching. She jets off down the stairs, sliding in through the slicing doors just as her music crescendos. Adrenaline and notes pumping through her veins, but it unexpectedly stops.

She looks at her phone, assuming her headphones got disconnected. The screen flashed with the icon of an incoming call; it was her mum. Answering reluctantly, hearing her demanding commands and responding with,

"Ok, mum."

She is lost in a trance to the rhetorical impositions, but something catches her eye. A child attempting to climb the seat like he was rock climbing. He kept trying, no matter how hard the train rattled him off course whilst his mother mindlessly scrolled on her phone.

The train stopped abruptly, and the child's hope popped like a bubble and crashed into seven finance guys like the 2008 recession. Whilst everyone was gasping. She burst out laughing.

Charity Shop - A Final Destination by Annabella

Strips of flowered fabric pushed together like pleats
Each a slight variation on a floral theme
Each bought to help celebrate in a hall to dance in
To twist and twirl
To match lipstick to
To frame hair, permed and set
So that it never moved or needed brushing

One day maybe soon these dresses
Will be plucked from those low rails
Folded into neat squares and rehoused
In ugly black plastic bags
Taken with all the memories they made
To a faceless place
To be selected or rejected
Their stories lost.

Untitled Haiku by Diane B

Drip drop drip drop
Water drizzles overhead
On the nose, umbrella up

Untitled One by Ruth G

It's hard to focus when feeling restless all the time
I try to contemplate life standing still for a while

I have difficulty concentrating
even among the calming trees
This mindfulness is hard to find outside or inside of me

I don't know if it's ADHD
or something else inside of me
I can't be motionless while the world is spinning around

Sometimes I wonder if I were a tree
Would I have less stress or suffer from ADHD?

Who knows but for sure I would be less dizzy,

افتخار توسط آرش نیرومند

هزاران سال
میلیون ها نفر
میلیون ها عشق
میلیون ها آرزو
هزاران جنگ
هزاران طوفان
هزاران صلح
آمده اند و رفته اند و خواهند آمد.
در آغوش تو
در سایه تو
که با شاخه هاي سرسبز و حاصلخیز خود پناه دادید
شما غذا می دادید، شادی، امید، زندگی و شادی می دادید
شما خاطرات ما را خلق کردید
شما با ریشه های بی شماری ریشه دوانده اید
تو هر زمان به من آرامش می دهی
همه جا
ای درخت قدرتمند،
ای وطن من.

Proud by Arash Niroomand

Thousands of years
millions of people
millions of loves
millions of longings
thousands of wars
thousands of storms
thousands of peace
have come and gone and will come.
In your arms
in your shadow
whom you sheltered with your green and fertile
branches
You fed, you gave joy, hope, life, and happiness
you created our memories
you rooted with countless roots
you give me peace anytime
anywhere
O mighty tree,
O my homeland.

Inanimate Objects Sitcom by Kit McDade

Would a cup of scalding tea
Thank the coaster for protecting
The wooden table beneath
From its heat?

Does the less used parts of the couch
Berate the favoured recliner for being
Sunken from overuse?

Do the bifolding doors
Wait in great anticipation
For the hot summer days
When we finally open them wide?

Does the TV get annoyed with me
When I forget to turn it off by the plug?

Do the stairs get together for a weekly meeting
To discuss what to do about the cats scratching
Them so often?

Do the skinner knives boast proudly
That I favour them the best?

The Ride by Arthur Stanfield

Look at past events. They are now history.
My tale. My story. My life.
Seated in the centre, keeping watch.
I do not allow them to take charge;
these dangerous demons can circle and develop.
I exorcise myself with holy water.

The birds in the air, the sun in the sky.
The drains in the pavement, the beggar on the corner.
All these are there every day, no exceptions.
They make up this cube which is square, and solid.
A jeweller offers bright light. A bus conductor offers
a way out.

I try not to sprint. I try to walk calmly,
You see it is never that simple

It is not all that it seems.
A quiet, fond dismissal,
the tear in the eye being magnified.

Cash in Marylebone by Webster Forrest

Marylebone station. High walls of sandstone in a slightly rosy shade supported an expansive awning of Victorian steel girders. Here on the inside of the station are arched stone doorways and lintelled windows peeping down onto the concourse. It feels as though someone had come along and put a roof of vaulted girders over a posh high street.

I looked at my watch. Ten to. I was meeting enebene99, who had the night before placed the winning bid on my old twin lens reflex. We decided to meet because I liked the idea of ready cash, and he liked the idea of getting the camera right away. No waiting for the postman. I knew what he looked like because I'd stalked him online for a few minutes after seeing his name and address.

My phone pinged, WhatsApp. It was from him. (I'd added him to my contacts so I could see what his WhatsApp profile pic looked like. It was a cat.)

'Running late, should be there by ten past. Sorry - Oli'

Oli Matthiesson. Educated at St. Martin's School for Boys in Wrexham. Briefly attended School of Creative Arts, Wrexham University before dropping out. Currently enrolled in Art History at KLC.

Enebene99. I'd looked that up too. It was the title of a movie from the Czech Republic. I wondered what the connection could possibly be between this film and this young chap who'd bought my old camera. Old camera, young guy, film from another country made the year he was born. Art student. Perhaps it was an art film.

There was a bench at the far end of the concourse. Next to a little coffee shop opposite the Boots. I headed in that direction, hoping nobody would get there before me. The only alternative to that nice, wooden, bench would be rows of metal benches where I'd a) freeze my backside, and b) have to sit in close proximity to other people. I'd reply when I reached the bench.

A Japanese man began moving towards the bench, away from his wife and daughter who were picking through greeting cards. There was no time to lose. I increased my pace. Fortunately, the man's wife called him over and he did not sit; I arrived just in time to prevent anyone else taking the seat. It was a two-seater, so technically I was not a hundred percent in the clear, but I sprawl myself out a bit and put my bag down beside me. Anyone wanting to sit next to me on the bench would need to ask, and I knew that would eliminate a certain percentage of potential bench-nabbers.

Once I was securely seated on the bench I took out my phone and replied, 'no problem - on bench next to Boots.'

Enebene99 was coming in from Birmingham, so I wondered why he'd only sent that message in the last five minutes. Surely he would have known that he was on a train that would arrive late. Perhaps he was with someone who had so occupied his attention that he completely forgot to update me on his ETA. I flipped through a few websites trying to find whether the train he was on was delayed, but there were so many cookies, and I had to register, and there was an app involved, and I didn't want any of that. So I just sat and waited, convinced that this Oli Matthiesson was going to be a twat.

Of course, in the old days I could have asked the Station Master; I wondered whether such a person even existed anymore. Doubtless I'd end up going up to someone decked out in lanyards and clipboards only to be told to look it up 'on our website'.

I looked at my watch. Five to. Fifteen minutes before he gets here, and then he'll have to wander around trying to figure out where the Boots is and where I am.

I just thought, 'there's so much crap we do in life and in the end, we're just going to die anyway so why the fuck bother?'

As I sat contemplating the absolute and sheer pointlessness of it all, I was interrupted by someone on my left who'd appeared from behind me, from the western end of the station.

"Hi."

I looked up.

"Oli." he said and extended a thin hand for me to shake.

I was in a quite sedentary position and could not simultaneously shake his hand and stand up. I didn't want to shake his hand while seated because it made me feel old. I didn't want to be rude and not shake his outstretched hand. In the end, I took his hand, and stood up at the same time, which I found he seemed to think was my asking for help in getting up - which he gave me, even though I was not trying to… anyway, in the end he helped me up and then I stood staring at his face while my mind turned to jelly.

I wanted to ask him to sit down - there were so many things I wanted to tell him about the camera: its quirks and all the things I'd learned from using it - how to use it well and get the best results. In the end, he was in a hurry and he just wanted to give me the cash and get on with his day, which was full of activities in a tight schedule, it seemed.

I stayed where I was on the bench after he'd left. I had his money in a pocket across the chest of my wind breaker. It was one of those three-quarter zip wind breakers that has a front pocket with a horizontal zip. That's where the cash was.

There were a lot of people in the station now and I wanted to get out of there. A certain heaviness kept me from moving for some time during which I again went over the things I would have told him about how to use the camera. All the secrets I'd learned through experience and reading. Knowledge which now had no purpose.

Creative Writing by Leslie Aldridge

Creative writing, a time to release tension
In writing whatever you mention
A poem or a story,
Keep adventures in your glory.
Enjoy putting words on paper
You can formulate them later.

Maze of Thoughts by Annabella

Being conflicted
seems to be a recurring theme in this life
It is, it isn't
I do, I don't
I care, I care less
Nothing secure or strong enough
to hold me during the doubt
Nothing that is mine
Nothing that I can call mine
When did I ever have such a thing?
Not to 'own', that wouldn't be right
Just someone who cared enough
 to be there for me, to hold me when it gets dark

My Body Is by Kit McDade

My body is an ancient Greek vase
How is it anything other than art?
Why have we been told to be like
A skinny vase?
To take up less space
To be afraid of our curves
Rather than show them
The reverence they deserve
I will not tame down my beauty
I will not modify my silhouette

An Apartment on 8th Avenue by Mark Holder

It's raining cats 'n dogs 'n frogs
Umbrellas up dodging the Broadway masses
But as the light dims Radio City music hall
glows in neon

We dive into a dive bar
for shelter and bourbon (When in New York)
Then dine in a diner
(pastrami on rye with a side of fries)

From every angle the sight of the tall elegant Empire
State beaming out light in the dark calls us home
(we're staying close by)

Tomorrow is Brooklyn and the forecast is dry

Somewhere Safe by Tom Mallender

A: I swear it was right here a second ago.

B: Don't tell me you put it in a safe place.

A: Oh no.

B: You didn't.

A: I think I remember seeing it and thinking I had better put it safe so I don't lose it.

B: Oh.

A: But then I am sure I would think not to do that.

B: Really?

A: Let me check.

B: Do you have a spare?

A: Yeah, I've bought loads as I can never find them, they are all somewhere safe.

B: Lost, you mean?

A: Temporarily unlocatable but not lost.

Casos e Acasos by Marcela Fontes

No teu caso,
não faças caso—
que o descaso
não vem ao acaso.

Bem que ao acaso
nem tudo tem caso.
Não faças do (a) caso
o meu caso.

Cases and Coincidences by Marcela Fontes

In your case,
don't make a big deal of it—
because the lack of care
doesn't happen by chance.

Well, not everything has a chance.

Don't make a big deal of it,
my case.

Becoming Young by J. H. Frost

When I am young,
I want to be there for myself.
I will speak gently
to the boy who checks his reflection—
not for admiration,
but for the approval he never found.

I'll sit beside him on that crowded train,
feeling the sway of the carriage,
noticing how he tucks himself in—
knees tight, elbows drawn,
as if shrinking might create a space of his own.
I'll remind him:
you don't owe silence
just to be seen.

When I am young,
I will not fear the eyes of others.
I'll wear the shirt
that makes me feel like shining.
I'll dance in the kitchen
to songs only I can hear.

I'll laugh, wide-mouthed and unsymmetrical.
I'll try things I might fail at—
hell, I'll try things I'm certain to fail at.
I'll write bad poems and share them.
I'll write good poems and share them.

I'll learn to say no
without torturing myself to give a reason,
and pat my own back for being so brave.
I'll sip caffé mocha at noon,
and go on an adventure without guilt.

When I am young,
I won't waste hours wondering
if I'm too much, or not enough.
Instead, I will be full
with soft rebellion,
with questions I never dared to ask,
with colours that make me laugh.
Let age come later.
For now, I shall choose joy
and walk back towards it.

Haiku by Barbara L

Drops of dew slip down
a blackberry tossed around
by harsh strong gales. Night

My Last Sunset by Kaze S

Antalya could no longer hear the Terminator robots hunting her. Looking at the forest in front of her, a path revealed itself amongst the small bushes competing for sunlight against the towering trees. Hurrying down the path, she soon found a secluded wooden house. Desperate for help, she raced towards it, feeling every small rock under her thin-soled shoes.

    Standing on the porch, Antalya clutched the handrail, gasping for air. She knocked once.
Deep in the forest, the snapping of a branch echoed. The robots were close. Antalya banged on the door. With no answer, she twisted the rusty handle, pushing the creaky door.

    "HELLO... hello?" She called out.
    No response.
    She walked over the carpet, barely covering the cold floor. Adjacent to it was a bookshelf filled with thick history books, sorted by author. One book stood out—Rose in the Blitz. Of all things, her favourite childhood book nestled among a shelf of dusty tomes. Inspecting it, she remembered reading it before the war, recollecting that there was always hope. Something fell from the book and clanged against the floor. Looking down, it was a key.

    Antalya placed the key in her pocket and ascended the stairs to a shut door. It wouldn't open. She bashed herself repeatedly against the stubborn door. The soldier fought on, but something dug into her leg.

The key had pierced her trouser pocket, almost whispering her next move, and it fit perfectly.

She opened the door and was met with a transcendent sunset through an obliterated window. A warm, fuzzy orange sun mixed with indigo, granting the night to overcome. With good in the sky, yet below lay the horror.

Beneath was her town, littered with corpses, innocent lives taken because of Keon Lumnis, a lonely scientist, bullied his whole life; on January 25th, 2078, he had decided to fight back.

Antalya turned around to find a rocking chair; its seat littered with broken glass. She raised a foot and swept the sharp remnants aside with her shoe before sitting down. Watching the sunset, she rocked back and forth, feeling glass shards crush beneath her. She looked at the mountains of bodies and blamed herself, thinking of everyone she had lost, everyone she owed. Her eyes started to water, blurring her view of the sunset.

Wiping her face quickly, looking at her favourite book, reinstalling a silver hope that there was someone else out there too. Antalya dashed out of the room, leaving the key still in the lock, halfway downstairs— she stopped.

She ran back to the window, capturing the magnificent view, and the wind gently breezed past her, guiding her path. Antalya ran back downstairs clutching the book.

The front door was still open. The sunset peeked through tall trees as bushes swallowed the last light. But... They were there, three robots ready to kill her. As she blinked, a bullet sliced through the air and pierced her heart. Antalya crashed to the floor with the book in her hand. The only memory that flashed before her eyes was that sunset.

Untitled #3 by Diane B

Winding through the flowers
All in rows
Hands out to touch as many
As you can like a game
Tall and reaching for the sky
Faces raised up to feel
The glow of the sun
Each flower alone in its place
Together
A group in silent chorus
When the wind blows whistling
Around and through the rows
Birds fly high
Do they use you to guide them?

Pigeon on the Pond - Gunnersbury Park by Salma A

Pigeon perches on the ledge,
clocking left and right at the writers ahead.
"Are you writing about me? Looking so serene.
This really is quite the unusual scene.
Away from your screens, staring up at the trees,
being so at ease, surrounded by the bees.
I must admit, here is far better than the streets!"

Trauma by Leslie Aldridge

Trauma does not rub off with bleach
Its memories not out of reach
It remembers days, months and even years
It rewinds and replays fears
Be kind to its numb needs
When we be patient and let it breathe
It's ok to say
I need help to get through the day.

There's a Saying… by Annabella

If I had a flower for every time
you made me smile
or laugh
I'd have a garden to walk in forever

But if I had a rock for every time
you made me worry
or cry
I'd have a cave to get lost in

The difference is, I have learned how to find a way out
that hasn't broken hearts

مرحبہ سے الوداع تک — عائشہ نور

مرحبا سے الوداع تک
ساتھ ساتھ جڑے ہیں
مرحبا اور الوداع
مرحبا وہ دن ـکہ آئے صدیوں کے انتظار کے بعد
مرحبا وہ گھڑیاں جو بیت گئی اچانک سے
زندگی کی پہلیاں، دھوپ چھاؤں
کاش کہ ایک لمبا دن ہوتا

From Welcome to Farewell by Aisha Noor

Welcome and farewell are linked together
Welcome that day that came after centuries of waiting
Welcome those hours that passed suddenly
The first moments of life, the sunshine and the shadows
I wish it was a long day

Third Date Woes by Kit McDade

Time is running out for a happy ending
Why does your hand not reach for mine?
We've reached the expiration date
Error: Spark not found
So now it's back to swiping
Back to shallow judgements
And talk, oh so small
But it's also another chance
At first date nerves
A chance to wipe the slate clean
To find the person who fans the spark
Into a flame
Who reaches for my hand every time
Whose first kiss will erase any doubts
From my head
About my attractiveness
Or whether I'm worthy enough to date
Who kisses me with the promise
Of a thousand more

For Decoration Only by Mark Holder

The grass has been cut and it does my nut
I can't smell it

The flowers are in bloom but I'm feeling the gloom
I can't smell 'em

The aftermath of rain in a green country lane
No—nothing

Spring lambs and cows too in a field full of poo
Glad I can't actually

See I've no sense of smell but I'm not bothered—well
This nose is for decoration only

5pm Rush Hour by Yaiza Freire-Bernat

Hammersmith Broadway at the 5pm rush hour, I think I want to barf. I brace myself as I spot the multicoloured ring in the distance and wonder what London would be like if no pedestrians paid attention to the traffic lights as they do in the crossing just before the entrance.

Standing at the crossroads I take a breath as a stampede of people make their way straight for me. I am quite literally getting lost in the crowd. Hundreds of people skimming past me. I close my eyes trying not to explode, it's like I'm a pinball in a never-ending machine waiting for the drop. I haven't even made it into the entrance yet! As I feel the stampede stop, I'm stuck in the middle of the road horns blaring telling me to get a move on. The panic is rising dangerously high so I run as fast as I can into the station before another tsunami descends on me.

Quick through the barriers. Oh crap, my bag is stuck! As I try to pull all I can hear are the constant bleeps of people tapping in and out. I pull a third time as hard as my non-athletic arms would let me and hallelujah it's free but onto my bum I fall and I hear a group of teenagers laughing.

"Bro did you see that!"

My face goes tomato red and I hold back the tears stinging my eyes. I run straight to my platform and I'm relieved that the train has pulled up. I jump on and burst into tears. Why does commuting have to be so stressful?

"The next station is Baron's Court."

Fuck's sake, I've gone the wrong way. I sob with full snot pouring down my nose and I have no tissues, so I do what you get told off for when you're a kid wiping your nose on your sleeve.
    I take a deep breath and concentrate on the slow rocking that I always find soothing. I feel my pulse lowering and my chest freeing up.

It's going to be ok.

Advice by Annabella

Look after your mind
You can't see it but
It's more important than any bone

You can't see it but
It does much harm if left neglected
It begins to feed on the bad stuff
And then you believe the lies it taunts you with…

That you're not loved
That you don't have any friends
You're weak
Not good enough
You're on your own

Should you see a glimmer of light
Protect it, tiny though it may be at times
Allow it to grow stronger to give you the energy
To withstand the dark moments which arrive
The dark moments that hope to settle down and start
Making a home in your head

The light can be shared by a smile from a stranger
A kindness done for you or by you
Always head for the light
In the daytime be with nature
In the nighttime with the stars

Changing the Bed by Pam Innes

Oh, how I longed to have my own bed!
Sharing with my sister could be chaotic.
Light on, I want to read.
Light off, I want to sleep.
At home I was no. 3 in the queue for a bed
(Please hold)

Whoosh…

Fast forward to my first flat.
Not just a bed, but a whole flat to myself. Bliss!
Sunday lie-ins reading the papers.

Whoosh

Fast forward to the fun of sharing the marriage bed.
Longing to go to bed. Joy!
Sunday lie-ins without the papers.

Whoosh…

Fast forward to the divorce bed.
Dreading to go to bed. Insomnia!
Nightly lie-ins, no sleep, no papers.

Untitled Two by Ruth G

I was looking for peace but all I found was chaos
Packed and noisy, there was no place to be quiet
The sun was out and so was the bourgeois
Who filled the park and set the prices
And even the tree shadows were all occupied
Where toilets are only available for 50 pence
No working men can get a shadow

Yesterday's Yearnings by Arthur Stanfield

I want to arrive at a scenic coastal beach.
I want to feel that all things are within easy reach.
Playing quietly.
Observing the waterfall at all times.
Toying with music—making sure everything rhymes.
Delusions of grandeur—don't we all have some of these?
The delicate leaves falling from the branches of the trees.
The curious mystery that will humble any man.
Striving to achieve—doing what we can!

Deep within the cave are all the answers known.
Trying to feel alive—trying to get in that zone.
Individuality I'm afraid comes at a cost,
It is the cross you bear when you never look lost.

John Coltrane by Chris Bird

Midnight glimpses round,
Smoking down,
Dripping from his skin comes the shade,
The cigarette haloes blow away,
And the saxophone glistens,
Like a sharp smile of joy.

He breathes,
Cool as dusk, soft as ashes,
Blowing crystal, glinting, scolding,
Streaming against drum beat pour.

New night sky colours flowing,
Riot blossom of light,
Scattering jade and turquoise.

And the man,
Like a statue in spellbound blue,
Just looks,
Silent and distant,
As the cloudy moon.

The Sounds Around by Taj Singh Puri

There's chirping from bushes,
small birds with their songs.

There are ocean-like waves,
it's the wind in the trees.

Then there's the hum of distant traffic,
an occasional heavy truck roll.

Through clear, blue skies up above,
a distant plane streaks quietly by.

Though all this is out there,
the fridge now grumbles to be heard.

Then gives up again,
and slow silence returns.

Untitled #4 by Diane B

Hope can be a light within
Hope can be a sign outside
Hope can be a beacon shining
to help show you a way
Hope can be just a 4 letter word
that has no meaning at all
Hope can be the only thing
you take with you at all
Hope can be something that grows
or diminishes like a flame
Hope can shine in your eyes
or mask a blemished sight
Hope can linger in your heart
and keep your spirit high

The Popping Parade of Popcorns by Aisha Noor

The days were long and boring
for the lonely only child
"Mother, please play with me!"
After they had played,
tired of make-believe friends.
Mother, always busy, non-stop chores.

"Come, Mama," says her fragile cry,
"Let's fly the swings and race the sky."
But Mama's hands are full of days,
of bills, of chores, of faded praise.
No play, always cooking, cleaning, plus much more.

Mother, please take me to swings in the park,
I wish I could play with kids while you're around.
Promises, promises never to be kept.
Fed up eventually, alone she left.
Standing alone by the popcorn lady,
the flame under her Karahi.

A hush of wonder in her eyes—
Where tiny orange seeds once lay,
now white-winged dancers rise.
They leap with laughter from the hot sand.
They whirl and twirl and cheer.
A chorus crisp with caramel notes
that only a tiny heart can hear.
One pops high and spins midair,

a bold little spark of glee,
another somersaults with flair—
Could that one be me?

She sees not snacks in sizzling sand,
but children freed from shells,
their fluffy feet tap rhythms sweet,
like magic casting spells.

Mesmerised, she clasps her little hands—
no claps, no crowd—
just steam and shadows near,
yet in their frolic she feels found.
A joy that draws her near.

They sing without a song to know,
They dance without a floor,
and she—so still, so tucked away—
wants nothing more.

To pop, to leap, to join their mirth
To be one in the bloom—
A popcorn child upon the Earth,
unfolding from her gloom.
She stood there, thinking she was one of them
One wears the colour tangerine,
one floats upon a trampoline.
They clap when she declares her plan—
to push the swings without a hand.

Popcorn lady was selling them,
two handful for one Anna.
Kind she was, a motherly face
Gave her some free to eat.

The lanterns blinked like sleepy eyes.
The sun waves goodbye.
The air was thick with jasmine sighs.
Popcorn lady completes her day.
Departing soon,
she viewed her young companion.

While somewhere deep in woven thread,
her mother woke with a heart like lead.
No sound, no cry—just rustling burqa,
a shroud of blue, a silent oath.

She swept through streets in ghostly grace,
her anger masked, her covered face.
She found her girl eating popcorn,
hands in dust, no hint of dread—

Then from the folds, a sudden grip:
a firm command through fingertip.
No voice, no scold, no angry yell,
but arms that held like storm in shell.
She pulled her close beneath the veil
where love and fury softly flail.

Inside the home, she took off her niqab.

"How come you walked with me?
You did not know I was your mother?
Why are you so silly,
leaving house muted as a mouse,
accepting popcorn and following a stranger in me?
You were unaware of the individual concealed beneath
the burqa or niqab.

"Hear, then, learn mother's words:
Do not walk blind through what you see.
No face, no heart, no hidden thread
should lead your steps unless you've read
what lives behind the gaze, the tone
A mask can smile and still be stone."

Then, maybe she was too young
to grasp a message so deep.
Always remembers Mother's words,
only after being deceived.

Haiku 1-3 by Pam Innes

The cool fan swivels,
Hovering over the ice
Yearning for Winter.

*

Chicken, fish or duck?
Twitching in her happy place
Dreaming of Dreamies.

*

Leaves come twirling down
Coloured carpet on the ground.
Happy feet! Stamp! Scrunch!

Time Travel by Maria Davis

"That's me when I was a child?"

"Don't be ridiculous, that picture is over 100 years old, and the kid is wearing shoes too big for his feet."

"I borrowed them."

"It's not you."

"No, it is."

"Prove it."

"Ok, in a few days I will time travel again, and when I arrive in 2190, there will be no more people."

"How is that proving anything?"

"Ok, next week you're having a nose job."

"What the actual…? How do you know about that? No one knows about that!"
"Because you posted your new nose online 6 weeks later, saying it was the best thing you've ever done."

"It was? It is? Hey, wait, what do you mean there are no more people? Where did they all go?"

"I have no idea, I freaked out and came home, now the Time Bureau are inching me forward to find clues."

"And have you?"

"No, but I have to say your new nose does look good, just don't have the lipo because you don't wake up from it."

"You mean I die!?"

"Your family donated your organs, so in a way you didn't."

"Should you be telling me this?"

"Probably not, but since we are all going to disappear in less than a century, I hardly think it matters anymore."

"But now I know, what about this timeline?"

"Well, if I travel again, there is a possibility you won't remember this conversation."

"No, my new nose," she says, looking in the mirror.

"Can you at least remind me again?"

"I have; this is the third time we've had this conversation."

Coming of Age by Kit McDade

We swap glow-in-the-dark stars
To the glow of our mobile phones
We swap dreams to harsh realities
From drawing on our lil kellies
To running a 10k
From whimsy
To the pragmatic
From believing in the tooth fairy
To bowing to late-stage capitalism
But we can still stick glow-in-the-dark stars
To our ceiling
We can dance in the rain
And we can seek out joy

Staring Out Over the Sea by Leslie Aldridge

Staring out over the sea
Brings thoughts of my past to me

The sun shining down bearing heat
Where the water and sun meet

We sailed into the dock; the sea was clear.
Lives were cherished with plenty of cheer.

The ship steered into the sunlight
Sailors standing to attention in all their might.

As we came to reconnect with loved ones,
The harbour was packed with wives, daughters and sons.

Home at last, our journey was complete
Leaving photographic memories for me,
Staring out over the sea.

The Unexpected Chord by Mark Holder

It's a chord change that does it
Something that gives me a feeling in the pit of my
stomach

It's not necessarily a major to minor thing or vice-versa
but maybe an unexpected chord that breaks up a
familiar progression and knocks me sideways

The other thing that happens (not always) is when I'm
singing along or trying to harmonise to a song—
when I hit a sweet spot I can find myself
on the verge of tears (of happiness I think)
I don't know why

This is what music does to me and will continue to do
always and forever

About the House by Siân-y-Blewyt

Toothpaste makes me hungry, no matter what I do,
20 minutes after brushing, only a piece of toast will do.

The cold water bottles must be moved in order,
from left to right of rack.
If you want a happy host, be sure to put them back.

I have a place for everything,
I need to know where things go—
so if you borrow something & don't return it,
be sure that I will know.

I'm a deeply private person
and dislike my views being shared,
without specific permission,
it very much breaks a code.

But I'm also really quite forgiving,
so don't worry if you mess up.

I'll likely forget all about it tomorrow,
it's peace I crave most.

But if you want me in my happiest place,
please be a thoughtful guest.

Rituals—Balance by Annabella

Brentford walk or stay indoors
one step at a time
on pavement, cold on my face
moving forward and seeing
stopping to look
sometimes intently
noticing the curve of petals
the point of leaves
colour
the redness of red, the green-ness of green
naming the shade
getting close enough to notice a scent
making time for a memory to energy
an experience
that is enough

Ravens by Marcela Fontes

The raven's shadow,
Flying high and low,
Spreading its wings
Far and near.
Casting a shadow,
Leaving a print—
An image,
A story
Behind.
Flying low,
Far,
Near and far.

It Was Red by Taj Singh Puri

Raphael was the best Turtle,
So my first bike— the brakes broke—
It was red.

Alvin the best Chipmunk,
My school lunch box—jam everywhere—
It was red.

Jason was the best Power Ranger,
Christmas toy car—Dad stepped on it—
It was red.

But Leon was my best friend in class,
he made me consider
something else instead.

Once, after his headaches left him,
he shared his favourite colour
—it was new!

And all I could think in return was:
"Why on God's green earth,
would anyone like blue?!"

As the years rolled on,
Blue calmed me down.

And red—I began to realise—
represented my frown.

They say it's a sign when you wear a red tie.
RED says a lot.
I was Jekyll and Hyde.

Blue was the colour that I've honestly tried, but
RED RUM RED RUM
There is a monster inside.

Listen Without Prejudice by Pam Innes

"It came from Epictetus."
        "You can get a cream for that."
                "What did?"
"Chris Hoy's aphorism."
        "You can get a cream for that 'n'all."
                "Ooh, er, get her."

T'was ever thus.
Somehow, talking about Greek philosophers
(Actually, he was Turkish.)
or Shakespeare, or ancient history
is seen to be showing off
or getting above your station.

For years I accepted it
Put my mask on,
hid my knowledge like a light under a bushel.
[Sermon on the Mount, Matthew 5:15, New Testament,
King James' Bible.]

I've read Epictetus' Enchiridion.
        "You can get a cream…" "Stop it!"
It doesn't mean I'm posh
or snobby, or arrogant.
Anyone can read his work.
After all, he was a slave
Admired for getting above his station.

What Does It Mean That "Out of the Abundance of the Heart the Mouth Speaks" (Luke 6:45)?
by Siân-y-Blewyt

Out of the mouths of babes,
or the abundance of the heart,
we speak.
And listeners retreat.
Or gather 'round.
It very much depends,
on what you put out.

Missed Flight by Salma A

I'm late to catch my plane. This isn't the first time. It's like an internal malfunction. Something not wired quite in tune with the rest of the world. Like there's a small snail-sized clock operating in my brain. Frantically, I look up and lock eyes with the man standing at the information desk. He looks calm and considerate, no signs of frantic chaos; I guess you've gotta be pretty calm to work at an airport. As I approach the desk his demeanour changes. I have that effect. It's like a disease that spreads. Sometimes it's good, on a night out, when boredom plagues. But mostly, it's a nuisance to be so discombobulated all the time.

I quickly explain my tardiness and that I have a flight to catch in under 30 minutes, bags and all. He sнірs and stares at me deadpan.

"Do I know you from somewhere?" he utters.

Is he serious? This isn't the time for unfounded déjà vu games. I have a plane to catch! Though… he does look familiar. I study my insufficient memory trail, another curse of the buggered mind.

"I'm really going to miss my flight," I pronounce. He swishes his hands through his hair, flustered and looking rather faint. Suddenly, it clicks.

The Best Room by Barbara L

Warm golden light
Embraces me
Birdsong in the morning
Surrounds me
Lying safely in the arms
of my duvet
Wrapped in like a cocoon
A butterfly will rise

Conditional Attraction by Kit McDade

A bi man told me he'd only fancy me
on masc days
Do you only adore the moon when it's round?
Is a rose only beautiful until it starts to wilt?
You only see the caterpillar
But I've transformed into a butterfly
I am not a starter to sample
I'm the whole goddam meal!
You want plain glass
When I'm a stained glass window
A kaleidoscope of gender
Keep your conditional attraction
I'm both masc and femme
If that's too much,
Go find less

Dad Is in the Car by Webster Forrest

"Is he still out there?"

I looked. I wasn't sure, then I saw the small trail of smoke come up out of the car window. He was on the passenger side. Opposite side from the house.

Mom got up and came to the window. It was cold out, and you could feel it on the glass. She folded her arms then looked up at the sky.

A small puff of smoke came out of the car.

Mom went to the hall and started putting her boots on.

"Take your coat."

"I'm just goin' out there to ask him if he wants his dinner in, or out."

"Of the car?"

She looked at me. Her nose was a little open and her mouth was just a little to the side, and closed. There was a bit of a smile. She shook her head. (It was funny, but it was no joke.) She now had her boots on and a scarf. I handed her, her jacket but she just opened the door and walked out there.

I went back to the window to watch. She slipped just once on the path but didn't fall - just raised her arms up from being folded. She got to the car. As she was going round the front of it, Dad leaned on the horn and Mom screamed, threw her arms up, and almost fell on her ass. It wasn't funny but you had to laugh.

She looked into the car where Dad was. She had this playful smile on her face like, 'I'm gonna get you for that'.

She made her way skidding a little and got up to the car window. She disappeared out of sight as they spoke through the window. After a minute or so I saw her standing a foot or so away from the car, with a cigarette in her hand. I'd never seen my mother smoking before, but there she was.

She started back in a couple of minutes later. She was rubbing her upper arms and she crossed the road. I heard the very vaguest echo of a sound that was my Dad's voice. She turned around and they asked and answered a few questions then she continued back into the house.

As she was coming up the path looking all cold, she looked up at me with a sort of helpless grin and shook her head like, 'Can you believe this?'.

When she was back in the house there was a bit of bossiness about her, as though she were acting on orders and we better also obey. We were sent upstairs to tidy our rooms while she started making enough room in the kitchen to do her famous meatloaf special, which consisted of meatloaf served inside a sort of cocoon made of cabbage leaves smothered in red sauce. It was like one giant cabbage roll which she had Americanised based on a recipe passed down from her Polish great-grandparents that she said was a ridiculous amount of work compared to her version.

I came up and stood in the doorway. She was on the counter next to the eggs - that's where she had the shopping list pad hanging on a nail on the side of the cabinet. She was moving stuff around, there was a pen behind her ear, and a fresh pad of paper on the counter next to the eggs, regardless of the fact that the old one was right there on the nail. She was making a hell of a racket with the pans. I knew not to go in there so I just stood watching.

"Honey, go get me a brandy," she said over her shoulder. I spun on my heels with my arms folded and went. She was always like this when Dad was in the car like that.

After bringing her her brandy I went up to my room. She wasn't gonna be very talkative until she got that big meatloaf in the oven. Then she'd sit back and have another drink.

Up in my room I looked out the front window. There was the car, with the small drifting puffs of smoke. I thought about that car, which Dad rarely drove, and had had since he and my Mom were teenagers. I thought about him being in there, sitting on the opposite side of it so as not to be seen by any of us. And I thought of why he would stay there instead of driving away to park up somewhere if he wanted to be alone. But it was just my Dad's way of not leaving us undefended when he needed some time alone. He just sat there, perched on the fringe, on the lookout but on his own.

He was a very sane man, my Dad.

Four Haikus by Siân-y-Blewyt

Dawn after bad sleep
Full of anguish and remorse
Stomach churning pain

    *

Music once my heart
Touches a pain so deep
I can't bear to let it in

    *

Eyes cannot create purple
Mysteriously
We all hallucinate it

    *

Who I hoped to be
Seems always just out of reach
Little faith in change

The Secret Life of a Tree by Marcela Fontes

Majestic tree,
What secrets do you hold?
Majestic, tall tree,
Your strong torso
Sharing your branches.
High and low,
You hold fruits,
Leaves, birds in nests.
In season, you are reborn.
You change, yet you remain.
You drop your leaves, your colours—
You show your face.
Your bark reveals
Your wrinkles, your story.
With your feet,
Your roots grow and expand,
And touch others.
With your branches,
You reach out to the world.
You share ideas,
Thoughts and history.
You hold wisdom,
You hold secrets.
You hold
Knowledge.
You hold
Heart.
Majestic tree.

Seasons of Change by Maria Davis

Dictated by season or by an inner need to change
The floordrobe swirls. I have nothing to wear.

Should I even go and be judged to the edge
When pyjamas are happy to snuggle and veg?

Time, where does it go?
I should have started planning ages ago,
When going out seemed like a good idea
But now I have nothing to wear.

Haiku 4-6 by Pam Innes

Deep fog in the sky
Echoes the fog in my brain
Praying for rain.

*

The black dog hounds me,
Clouding me with depression,
Yet I still have hope.

*

How can I love me?
Self compassion therapy
Love without judgement.

The Soundtrack of Our Home by Siân-y-Blewyt

At 5am on Sundays
there's the rumble of a nuclear waste train

as it cruises under Brunel's three bridges,
passing our lovely home

(It's not too much of an imposition, given we're in
a no-drive through zone.)

The front door likes to slam,
the poppity ping often follows along.

Our fridge likes to hum to the back door chimes
(An improvised burglar alarm.)

All the while birds chirrup and cheep, as the cat
scratches to go out to prowl.

It's really rather quiet now
since the Metal went off to uni,

the Arianator will join him soon, & the BF's galumping
will be gone soon too.

Only the sacred choral remains, in a cacophony of
keyboard strokes and clicks.

The sounds of hoovering and cleaning will start fading
in consequence.

Stereophonic musivisual changes, mark a stereo to
monotonous tone.

Does Anyone Remember Uncle Holly? by Mark Holder

Waiting to see Santa in the Selfridges queue
Greeted by a character that nobody knew
Does anyone remember Uncle Holly?

From time to time, I'd mention his name
But from those I asked no acknowledgement came
Could it be I'd made up Uncle Holly?

Of course I didn't, my brother was there
A little younger than me and he remembers — Yeah!
That won't prove he was real though — Uncle Holly

Jen thinks we're Little Lord Fauntleroys
Seeing Santa at Selfridges like two posh little boys
Sometimes I wish I'd never set eyes on Uncle Holly

Then on a visit to Chiswick this Friday last
There in a cabinet protected by glass
A Selfridges badge with the face of Uncle Holly

Looks like WC Fields, me & Jen agree
And truth be told he's a bit creepy
But I don't really care, it's the proof it's Uncle Holly

The quest is over but it's tinged with sadness
I've loved the chase and all the madness
But I didn't make it up —
he was really real, old Uncle Holly

Co-Conspirators of Hope by Zaneta C

Co-conspirators of hope sounds Obama-like.

Like a line from one of his dope orations.

Co-conspirators of hope, an antidote for the nations?

Prisoners of hope, the good book says, a new iteration of the word *collaboration*—now an arty-farty term, replacing collusion with the Germans of old, once foretold.

Co-conspirators of hope.

Are we ready to take a bow and plough on?

Or are we ready for providence to have its course?

The Idea by Taj Singh Puri

Monotonous and dreary,
the day rolls on.
Grey clouds and dark skies
veil the itch from beyond.

But then, in an instant,
bright rays burst through.
"An idea! A fresh thought!"
Something brand new.

Quick: "A pen! Some paper!"
No time for that now.
Wait: "Use your phone!"
Just text it all out.

Brain dump in an instant.
No time to make sense.
"Wait! That's not right!
That bit should be past tense!!"

The details take over,
the idea slips away.
Now the sudden realisation,
" …wasn't that work meeting today?"

Two Friends Like the Same Person by Maria Davis

"I'm ordering a salad."

"You never order a salad."

"Yes, I know, but l met this guy and he's introduced salads to me in a whole new light."

"Oh really!"

"Yeah, he's like a vegan bodybuilder, you should see his muscles." Anna swoons, waving a fork in the air.

He's probably not as handsome as my crush, thinks Dianna.

"I've met someone too."

"You have? Oh, do tell."

"Yeah, he's a personal trainer at WikiLeaks, apparently the staff were getting stressed out, so management hired him to keep their minds active, he didn't say how, but it doesn't sound like fun."

"Wow, that's amazing, mine just got a new training job. I'm hearing about it later; he's taking me out tomorrow night."

"Where are you going?"

"Not sure, he said it's a surprise."

"Aren't you worried?"

"About what?"

"Going out on a date to an unknown destination."

"Well, I wasn't. Maybe I should give you his details and number so if you find my body next week, you can avenge my death."

"Dramatic much, but yes, ok."

"Sent."

"What the actual fuck!"

"What?"

"This is my guy l was telling you about."

"Ha ha!"

"No, really, he has the same name and number."
"Oh no. So now what? Do we both date him and let him pick or ghost him?"

"Ghost him, I say, that way we stay friends, and he gets to keep his salads all to himself."

"Waiter, can I change my order?"

Come on England by Pam Innes

Saints and bards top and tail our festivities
spanning the old and new years.

St Andrew brings in the winter festival–
an opening run to test our stamina.

Hogmanay picks up the baton,
with a simultaneous wake for the old year
and a rousing welcome to the new one,
leading us through January with waves of
reciprocal first footing to wish our loved ones
all the best in the coming twelve months.

January moves towards the festival's
Bardic conclusion on Burns' Night.
Rabbie's poetry and songs,
the ubiquitous haggis and whisky,
skirling pipes and swirling kilts…

Now, imagine if Rabbie had been born on
St Andrew's Day.
There'd be one mega fandabbydozy party!!

Happily, England has that wonderful serendipity…
and more.
23rd April is St George's Day,
Shakespeare's baptismal day
(and, allegedly, the day he died).

Sadly, the day passes by like a dreich Sunday afternoon.

Where are the celebrations,
the pomp and pageantry that England
is renowned for?

Come on lads and lasses! Gie it laldy!

A Familiar Conundrum by Yaiza Freire-Bernat

A: "You go ask them!"

B: "No you go!"

A: "I don't know them, it would be weird, you go."

B: "No, because they know me and it will be weirder."

A: "What if we go together?"

B: "Yea cause that's not gonna freak them out."

A: "Mmmm yeah I guess."

B: "Then what? No one goes?"

A: "What if we ask that guy to ask for us?"

B: "Yea all right."

Spiders by Lauren Storey

It crawls on the window display,
Weaving in and out of fabric,
As the only one unafraid
It's my job to go and grab it.
I bring paper and a glass
To take the poor spider outside,
I'm the only one in this shop
Not afraid to take it out alive.
Later that day a fly buzzes in
And I hide in disgust out back
I leave those bugs for my colleagues,
There's no way I'm dealing with that.
My colleague wafts it outside
And laughs at my horrified face
I hate it in the summer when those
Gross creatures enter this place.
I can deal with the ones that crawl,
I'll even deal with the ones that bite
But even if the bug is small
I can't deal with the ones that take flight.

Never Judge Books by Covers or Looks From Lovers by Clare Smith

Do you love me…
Do you pen windows to my soul
Chapters of unknown
Scriptures of sacredness
I'm yet to know…

Write me a love letter and a lullaby
So you can put me to sleep
After disappointing me.

Lull me into a false sense of security
Then discard me
So I can bleed out the drops of love for you
That filled my heart.

Close the curtain on the sunshine,
That was your smile.
Crush it quickly
Put it out of its misery.

If my heart could talk
It would tell tales of how fear turned into hope
And naively it trusted again and again.
Or maybe it would be mute
Burnt and left speechless from despair & deceit.

I went to visit the Redwoods.
Ground where we lay our foundations.
There, I laid upon the earth
Silently
I began to pray
Wishing that I'd sink,
Swallowed whole into the ground
Buried in the bereavement
Of us.

The Gender Euphoria of Vans by Kit McDade

Who knew stepping into
A new pair of vans
Would lead to me stepping
Into my true self?
How the black and white shoes
Would send my confidence soaring
How the extra height would
Feel like I walked amongst giants
How cosplaying as Nick Nelson
Would bring me closer to
A more authentic me!
These are more than shoes
They are keys to my soul
To my gender expression

To the kind of pure trans joy
That the media often misses
They support my feet
And express who I am inside
They take me places
And show me who I've always been

The Moment by Arthur Stanfield

He squatted delicately on the roof
of a farmyard building. Completely alone
knowing there would be no disturbance.

The scenery was so pleasing to him.
Loving the way the brambles had made
their home in a large rhododendron bush.

A few blackbirds flitted back and forth poking around
on the ground. Constantly alert.
Occasionally a rabbit would appear then vanish.

The sky was slightly overcast
Providing shade for his troubled mind
White puffs of cloud reminding him of the heavens.

He noticed the many different shades of brown
that he could see. The intertwining, weaving wood.
His head ducked slightly, humility consuming him.

And for one millisecond he glimpsed eternity.
Stillness and movement becoming one.
Inside and out mirroring each other perfectly.

The Light by the Sea by S. Ahmed

The last time I took the time to stop and reflect was on a trip to Whitstable on the Kent Coast.

It was an opportunity to notice the different blue shades in the sky on the horizon and ponder how the light reflected the sun, sea and sky.

If I had more time, I would paint a picture of the iridescent flakes of jade green and blue green shimmering in the waves in the expanse of sea.

And show the way the sand beneath changed the colour from a softer dark green to a lighter aqua green.

And then how the sea made the sky full of speckled colours of the rainbow, culminating in an overarching blue, full of light.

I smelt the fresh sea air and felt the breeze on my face. I was breathing deeply again and taking in all the benefits of water. I reflected on the light and felt lighter as they took the train back to London.

As the train pulled out, I thought, I'm glad I took the time to fully paddle in the cooling sea, feel the soft sand wash over my feet, and notice the maroon coral and forest green seaweed gently tickle my toes.

I felt a sense of calm. I noticed colours again.
I slowed down.

Tit for Tat by Webster Forrest

Our first date was at the symphony. Pictures at an Exhibition. My mother warned me that taking a girl to see something as needlessly dramatic as Mussorgsky was asking for trouble. I'm not sure what she meant by trouble, but if it was ninety seconds of intense over-the-sweater action in the concert hall fire escape then she was right.

   Our second date was a ball game, but since she didn't have any interest in baseball and my team struck out at every pitch it meant I was in a bad mood, and she was simply bored.

   That one nearly spelled the end of everything. But it was our third date when things got really interesting. I took her to the Aquarium. Now, I'd been obsessed with nature and animals and the living world my entire life, so I had all this public-television expertise on the subject, which she didn't have, because worms and molluscs weren't exactly her thing - she was more into history and law, which frankly I found, and continue to find, extremely dull. But there we were in the undeniably impressive setting of gigantic tanks of seawater and all manner of aquatic creatures from pufferfish to stingrays. And she really dug it.

   I suppose once you are put face to face with a thing it becomes more captivating than if you only see it in a book or on a television screen. It bears mentioning at this point that I had for several days now been in the habit of recalling to my thoughts the aforementioned sweater experience to the muffled strains of Pictures at an Exhibition, and not to put too fine a point on it, I was beginning to think of ways in which the experience might be repeated - perhaps with some variations which I shall leave to the reader's imagination.

It turns out that security measures to protect stingrays from the public and vice versa are far more stringent than those put in place to protect the safety and privacy of the nation's leading orchestral musicians, because try as I may, I could not find a fire escape which did not have a written warning on it outlining various fines and/or custodial sentences which one would flaunt even by opening the door in question, never mind going through it.

And so, we eventually found ourselves in the gift shop having seen all the deadly creatures and now being confronted with them anew, albeit in non-lethal plush form. She seemed to want me to buy her a narwhal pencil case. Instinctively I saw this as a test, both of my character and generosity, and also of her ability to get her way.

Well, I wasn't so callous as to view this in tit-for-tat form, though in a literal sense the comparison was exact. However, my instincts having been honed by my previous two dates, I followed my gut feeling and magnanimously bought her the pencil case and even threw in a silicone octopus that goes on the end of a pencil.

It turned out to be, as they say, a great romance. We saw each other on a regular basis for the next three years and she became my first serious girlfriend. It might have gone on forever if it hadn't been for the fact that we both bowed to our parents' respective urgings and chose the best universities for our chosen subjects of biology and law. We lost touch, and I have myself since married and had two wonderful sons. When I think of them not ever having been born it fills me with dread.

    Still, whenever Pictures at an Exhibition comes on the radio, I always think of a narwhal pencil case and the softness of a yellow mohair sweater.

Untitled #5 by Diane B

If the moon smiled
It would be a wide toothy grin

From way up high
Looking out and looking in

Shining a pathway
For a walk or a run

Shining an exit
For prey to run

Owls screech
Bats wings flap

If the moon smiled
It would be like a peaceful blanket
Underneath to rest and dream

Tempo by Marcela Fontes

O tempo que nada cura,
gente que passa—e deixa marca.

Deixa que te cure da gente
que, no tempo, marcou o tempo.

Tempo que gira,
que deixa que tudo volte no tempo.

Tempo que passa,
que leva,
que leva da gente,
que te cure e te deixe.

Te deixe em mim,
em ti,
em nós.

Tempo... tempo.

Time by Marcela Fontes

Time that heals nothing,
people who pass by—and leave their mark.

Let it heal you of the people
who, in time, marked time.

Time that turns,
that lets everything return in time.

Time that passes,
that takes,
that takes from us,
that heals you and leaves you.

Leave you in me,
in you,
in us.

Time... time.

Life's Journey by Maria Davis

Away we went on our mini adventure, car packed with
items that may never see the light of day.
The radio accompanied our every turn.
The sun danced around white fluffy clouds the whole
day.

Madonna's Like a Prayer, played the most that day.
And we sang and sang along, even over other songs,
our mantra of our time.

"Just like a prayer, I'll take you there."

Years have passed since, and friends have long gone,
new songs play on the radio, as I drive, kids screaming,
car packed with items I still may never use.
"Are we nearly there" begins the moment the car starts.
Then Madonna says she'll take me there, and I know it's
going to be a good day.

Refraining My Baggage by Kit McDade

I have my own baggage
Sometimes it weighs me down
But it's mine
It adds black to the canvas of my life
To make the stars shine!
My pain has given me empathy
And means I never take the good days for granted

To overthink is to overcare
A messy room is full of blessings
My short stature means I get
To rely on the kind help of strangers
To put my suitcase in the overhead
Lockers on the plane

My anxiety means for a rich imagination
That I can use to envisage a bright future
Rather than a dark one
My autism has given me
The ability to feel so deeply
And taught me the joy
Of making time for rest and ease

I used to want to escape my mind
But now I understand it
I accept it rather than rebuke it
I am pleased to be me
On this floating rock through space

Warm Embrace by Yaiza Freire-Bernat

I can feel their touch and imagine their arms
wrapped around me.
The tears streaming down my face
and the comfort of a warm embrace.

I can feel the imprint of each of their fingers
of their right hand on my shoulder blade.
Their left hand on my ribs keeping me safe
as I weep my sorrows away.

They are the only place I want to bury myself,
the person I want to spend my forever with.

Paparazzi by Zaneta C

If I could become a nice person, I would.

I have been chasing misunderstood celebrities, the best I can. A good paparazzi… the best stalker in the land.

The financial limbo that comes with being honest threatens to render me a penniless man.

It was my goal but snapping the latest Love Island star is now a new story told.
All that I've learnt is that it pays to be bold.

Harmonica by Lauren Storey

I remove the polished metal from its case
And bring the harmonica to my lips

The tabs are still fresh in my memory—
It took me a while to get to grips

with it, but now I'm ready to perform for you—
I play happy birthday then Blink 182.

What a fun skill this has been to pursue.

My Trusty Screwdriver by J. H. Frost

I
a case wide open—
one tool in a sea of parts
I know just where to start

II
metal danced all night
each screw a whispered promise
my world came to life

III
found again in dark
still sharp in its silent task
my old friend of steel

IV
window's stuck for years
one click one twist then it breathes
the air smells like change

Lionel by Mark Holder

On the last day of their holiday, they popped their final 20p in the slot and watched the grabbing tool bear down on the heap of soft toys.

They'd spent most of their spare change in the amusement arcade on the pier trying to extricate the small lion from its cage but this time it was looking more promising.

The grabber clung on to Lionel (as they had already christened him) and lowered him down to the exit chute and he dropped to the floor.

The couple could not contain their excitement, and when a grandfather walked past and told his toddler grandson to "mind that lion" in a Yorkshire accent, they knew that Lionel was real.

Oh, Milton, Where Art Thou? by Pam Innes

My garden was my happy place
Designed, constructed,
and tended lovingly by me.

Then everything crashed
and crushed me inside.
I withdrew into my home
in flight from my emotions.

It's like I cast myself out of my own Eden.
All my self-loathing
and lack of self-compassion
has become an invisible barrier.

Even though it's been years,
I still haven't been able
to go into the garden,
feeling that I don't deserve such happiness…

…and yet hope keeps me longing.

I dream to get back there,
as to some distant Shangri-La.
Regaining the earthly paradise that I lost.

Blossom Haiku by Kit McDade

Blossoms bloom at once
Beautiful bursts of beauty
Flash of blush then gone

An Ode to Peperoni Pizza by Kit McDade

Salt bursts on the tongue
river of gooey cheese runs
pepperoni crunch

Untitled #6 by Diane B

I go and lie down
        where the wood drake rests
The breeze gently brushes my face
        which is facing toward the sun
The soft velvet grass is my pillow
I can hear the water lapping
        at the edges
I rest in the grace of the world
        and I am free.

داركوب اثر آرش نیرومند

نشستن روی یک صندلی،
من اینجا گیر کرده ام
من دیگر نمی توانم پرواز کنم،
دیگر نمی توانم ببینم
پس من در خوابم یک رویا می بینم،
داركوب بودن من،
هر روز درختان را در آغوش می گرفتم،
من هر روز درختان را می بوسیدم،
داشتم می پرسیدم،
من به دنبال آن هستم،
قبل از غروب آفتاب به دریاچه نگاه می کنم،
در میان آغاز سایه های تاریکی،
شاید یک لحظه برگردم
پاییز گذشت،
من عشق خود را در میان رنگ های پاییز از دست داده ام و انسان شده ام.

Woodpecker by Arash Niroomand

Sitting on a chair
I'm stuck here
I can't fly anymore
I can't see anymore
So I dream in my dreams
I dream of being a woodpecker
I hugged trees every day
I kissed trees every day
I asked
I looked around
I looked over the lake before sunset
Among the beginning of the shadows of darkness
Maybe, maybe I'll come back for a moment
The autumns have passed
I've lost my love among the colours of autumn
and I became human.

Fallen by J. H. Frost

Broken wings of hope—
a parakeet has fallen
on autumn's cold stone

Cave by Annabella

A cave,
A place of safety, a shelter
A place I can be alone in
A place of silence

The foundations are important
I give attention to the support it needs
To remain a safe space
It's a place I can mould to what it needs to be
Sometimes the foundation shifts
But it is responsive to the care
I put into it
Its shape changes ever so slightly and that is good
So it grows and moulds to its purpose

A cave
A place of safety
A shelter

The Shoe by Leslie Aldridge

I'm a shoe, I come in a pair
My sole takes wear and tear
Me and my other shoe had a life in a box
Our life to fit feet in socks
We both have a fresh start
On a new journey we depart

Being Still by Marcela Fontes

Immobile.
Rested.
Breathing.
Feeling.
Seeing—observing.
Scent—smelling.
Hearing sounds, voices, thoughts.
The wind whispering
Small, little secrets.
Seeing—observing the surroundings.
Touching, caressing
The grass, the leaves.
Being still.
Immobile.
Rested.
Breathing.
Alive.

Untitled #7 by Diane B

I can feel your pain
I can feel your sorrow
I can sit with you
There is no judgement
There is no critique
We can share the things you want to
And avoid the things you don't
We can share through words or silence
Whichever way you choose
Compassion with a tiny bit of grace

The Wardrobe of Bess by Lauren Storey

There once was a woman called Bess
Whose shopping habits were a mess,
Each choice a mistake
And yet, she still ate;
Making ugly clothes look their best.

Everyday Magic by Maria Davis

The oven is mysterious,
Created goods, the centre focus of any dinner party
Except me, when I try, it's not arty

I should study chemistry
But it all seems overkill
When baked delights are made to perfection
Not even by human hands.
Made by a few lines of code
0's and 1's. That's art, that's an ode

Dementia Days by Annabella

Leave it, I'll do it better myself
You and that left hand
She didn't even notice I used knives, spoons, scissors,
handles
Using my right
Watching, always watching
Reminding to wrap the peelings
in just one sheet of newspaper
of which she had a pile at least 2 feet high
This she did until she was in her 90s
from her seat that reclined
but in which she would never relax
Then her mind got lost
trapped some place in her long past
Now she doesn't seem to care
She notices nothing
Days could all just be called this day, one day, some day
Miss you, Mum

I Left My Heart in Cyprus by Kit McDade

I left my heart in Cyprus
It's at the Kalifi beach bar
Where the iced coffee foam
Is like drinking a cloud
And the sea shines like a cut diamond

My heart is in my happy place
The wind whipping my hair
And the sun caressing my skin
I remember the clear water

Kissing the shore
Forever retreating and returning
In an ever flowing song

The sea cools my overheated skin
The salt melting on my tongue
As a wave makes an introduction
I dry off at my table
Kindle in hand
For once not wanting to escape
Into the world of the story
The landscape being beautiful
Enough to stay

I long to return to Cyprus
To reunite with my heart
And my mother's heritage
To where I feel whole
To where I feel at home

I Don't Like Being Me by J. H. Frost

I don't like being me.
I don't like my lack of confidence,
my doubts that scream louder in quiet rooms,
my fears that frequent me
when the world falls asleep.

I don't like how I stutter
when the right words slip away,
how I pretend to be happy
in front of faces that wouldn't understand anyway.

I don't like my inability to relax.
The way my body tenses,
always bracing for impact.
I don't like how I grow into laziness—
like holding onto a rope to escape,
only to slip further into the abyss.

I don't like
how I waste my own time,
bury my potential,
and burn out my gentleness.
I don't like being me.
But maybe,
maybe I haven't really been me.
Maybe I've only been surviving,
Masking the scars,
shrinking to fit all expectations,
to please everyone but me.

Maybe they don't know me.
Maybe I don't know me.
So I want to find myself,
not who I'm supposed to be
but who I really am—
the true me.
The one beneath the camouflage.
The one who remains, despite the noise.
The one who cries without fear,
acts with conviction,
and laughs without apology.

And someday,
when I finally find me—
the true me—
I think,
I'll like being me.

To conclude this anthology, we are incredibly proud to showcase the following preview sections of longer form pieces of work being written by Write-London participants for later publication/performance.

The following extract is from a novella sequence Webster has been working on over the last year which charts the path of a vampire though various time periods. This section of the story takes place during Mozart's visit to Prague in the 1790s.

Funeral by Webster Forrest

It was entirely the wrong season for a child's funeral.

The old man, crumpled and bent in his thick coat stood as upright as he could, but years of malnutrition combined with a bitter and pessimistic nature, had bent his body into a miserable crescent out of which he was never been to elongate himself.

The single horse-drawn conveyance looked more like a farmer's cart than a funeral carriage. It was completely open, and the simple coffin lay flat on its back like the dead boy it contained. One thoughtful man who worked in the undertaker's yard had had the sense and care to nail in some slats to the coarse wooden boards upon which the coffin lay, to prevent it sliding as the cart's old wheels jostled and tumblingly progressed over the sunken cobblestones on the lonely route from the undertaker to the Malostrana cemetery.

It was such a long and tiresome journey that the old man had been advised not to attempt it on foot. As a consequence, he was there early and stood waiting in the delicate spring rain which fell all day. His sole companion was his old friend Brodsky.

Finally, after what seemed like an eternity, the carriage conveying his son rattled through the cemetery gates. The priest had been hiding, or praying, or staying dry, in the chapel, so Brodsky dutifully went off to inform him of the arrival of the coffin.

Coach drivers have a certain kind of learned disconnection from the people and objects they convey. In this case, the person—or object—of the young man in the coffin was not mentioned by him.

Two gravediggers hovered nearby, leaning on the ends of their long shovels. They each had soft caps which were normally folded and stuffed into their back pockets. However, because of the rain neither man removed his cap when he came up to lift the coffin from the cart to place it next to the hole which had been dug in advance.

The priest came up. His long stoles fluttered at his sides in a manner which lent an air of ceremony to his otherwise sprightly gait.

Brodsky was kind enough to hold his own umbrella over the Father's head as he read words from his book which had been pre-ordained to be spoken at this child's funeral even before his birth.

"Blessed is the Lord, our God…"

Was that a sound?

"…Almighty and ever living God, remember the mercy…"

Brodsky was leaning forward with his ear aimed at the coffin. In so doing he inadvertently exposed the Father to some rain, which occasioned a loud clearing of the throat from the pious clergyman.

"…in this life. Receive him, we pray, into the mansions of the saints…"

It was at this point that there was a sound so loud which came from the inside of the coffin, that all present stopped what they were doing and instinctively leaned in to listen. Even the priest could not deny that something was amiss.

Coming from the inside of the coffin was a quiet humming sound, and a tapping. All leaned in. Was it singing?

Everyone looked to the priest, who cupped his ear, and leaned in to listen to the coffin. In an instant, a bony grey hand came through the wood and grasped the priest by the throat. He tried to get away, but the strength of that grip was superhuman, the choking effect so complete that the priest himself could not even emit a scream.

All present panicked and were thrown into a state of horror. With the gravediggers each using both hands to pull the priest off the hand that gripped his throat, the two older men tried to smash the coffin open with stones and a shovel.

The sight of the hand was horribly altered from how it had been in life or even in the early hours of death before the boy was put into his coffin. Instead of the delicate hand of a child, it had increased both in size and muscularity and was covered in long thick hairs like those on the back of a dog when it raises its haunches.

The priest's face was going purple, and the two gravediggers had managed nothing in trying to pull him off the offending hand. Pushing Brodsky aside, one of the gravediggers took up his shovel and, raising it high above his head, brought it down like an axe upon the bony wrist of that hand. The skin broke, and there was a cracking sound like a shingle snapping, but the death grip persisted. A second blow broke through into sinew and flesh, and the bony shape of it now had a deformed and inhuman appearance. A third brought another cracking sound. The arm itself was now at a sickening angle, yet the grip on the throat of the young priest was unyielding. Another blow, this time on the wood, broke through.

Suddenly there was silence except for the rain falling on the varnished wood, then, a long hollow wail so unnerving that it sent shivers down the men's backs.

One more blow of the shovel finally cut through, severing the hand completely. The priest fell back gasping for air—Brodsky kicked the hand away and bodily lifted the priest by the shoulders.

Out of somewhere, somebody produced a hip flask which with shaking fingers was quickly opened; all partook.

Finally, as the old man turned and looked with unbearable shame into the eyes his old friend, his stare moved from there to the ground where it became fixed on the hand, which now lay motionless with its fingers pointed up and its palm exposed to the rain. To everyone's surprise, Brodsky picked the hand up on his own, forced it through the hole that had been smashed in the coffin, and bodily took the priest by the shoulder and made him stand at post by the coffin.

All present except Brodsky began reciting the prayer, "Holy Mother of God, holy virgin of virgins, St. Michael…" while he solemnly recited some verses in Hebrew.

Finally, without waiting for the prayers to come to an end, the two gravediggers wasted no time in getting the coffin, and the prayer book, and a rosary, and the priest's crucifix all into the ground as fast as they could.

The rain, which had picked up during the attack, suddenly stopped as soon as the prayers were over, and a great light and warmth filled the area around them.

The five present exchanged looks, each crossing himself, including Brodsky for luck, and they all left that place by a different route and never spoke of it again.

The following is a preview of the upcoming novel *"Phoenix Star"* written by **T M Davis.**

Welcome to the future. Please comply.

When a reclusive detective accidentally kills a corrupt bailiff in self-defence, he uncovers a piece of forbidden military tech—and with it, a conspiracy linking a missing father, a tech giant, and the secret control of the nation's health.

It All Started When…

Saturday 7th August

PHOOW.
A sonic blast from the door sends tiny pieces of oak flying in all directions across the lounge area of number 9 as one of the Military agents separates the door from its lock.

The bailiff swings the broken door to one side, entering triumphantly, as another agent begins reciting the monotonous bailiff laws of 2097. Discarded food wrappers are scattered along every surface except for a computer gaming mat, branded Invaders From Mars.

The place looks like it had been turned over by another team, causing the bailiff to double-check his paperwork.

"Mr Sam Green, apartment 9." Says the bailiff to himself. Noticing a sleeping man buried under the duvet.

"Check he's breathing," he thunders to one of the agents.

The loud vocal droning must be coming from Invaders, is Sam's first thought, reasoning that the game is still running. So, with sore muscles, an aching back, and a definite hangover, Sam's gloved hand lands on the remote.

The bailiff, clocking the movement, shoots the weapon out of reach, triggering Sam's sleep device to start playing. As the device's volume and speed increase, all the Military agents freeze in place.

"What the fuck?" screams Sam, leaping out of bed seeing four Military agents frozen in place, just staring, but grabbing his immediate attention is a gun moving towards his head.

"Now, now, now! There's no need for that kind of language, I'm Argon Wainwright, your bailiff, here to collect because you haven't paid your bills," he declares, dashing his foot along the many cardboard boxes by a wall.

"You've got a lot of expensive toys."

"They're not mine."

"Oh, you stole them to fund your newfound lifestyle," he says, gesturing to the surrounding mess.

"Officially, I'm just here to document your belongings," he continues, waving a casual hand over the Military agents, "but as you see, my colleagues are taking a little break, so there's no one to stop me from kicking your stupid little head in. So why don't you save everyone's time, pay your fucking bill, the agency's fee, plus 5000 credits directly to me, for having to deal with your stinking arse, then I'll leave you, wearing your stupid gaming gear, to your miserable life," he finishes dramatically, returning his gun in place.

"They're not moving, what's wrong with them?"

"They're under my control and won't be waking until I decide."

"Sister?" says Argon picking up a framed photo from under a pizza box. "Oh, so you were banging her," he adds noting the pained look on his client's face. "I say 'were' cause obviously, you're not doing anyone now in the state you're in, you'd be lucky to get some paid action." He concludes by rubbing his crotch on the photo.

"Put that down."

"Shut it, you don't get to decide anything, you miserable piece of shit," says Argon lunging for a gut punch. Sam easily sidesteps slamming him with his shoulder, reeling him backwards. There is a massive cracking noise from the bailiff's head colliding with the corner of an oak cabinet, Sam returns to stance, readying himself for the next attack. It takes him a few seconds to realise the bailiff is not going to be moving… ever again.

The End of Death

Stuttgart, Germany, 8 years ago

"What a show I have, none of them have any idea how freaked out they're all going to be in under twenty minutes!" grinned Bernard van Housen, making one final adjustment to his tie, and entered the conference room.

The big screen on the back wall began his presentation as he scanned the expectant faces.

"Gentlemen, in front of you are agreements. Please read and sign; it guarantees your protection as much as ours and pledges confidentiality regarding today's proceedings," said Bernard as he watched everyone place their handprint on the tablets and sign their names.

"Jackson, step forward," he said as he put on a whiter than white lab coat, gloves and safety glasses.

Teal Jackson, relatively new to the company, was elated at being summoned by the top boss and, after several conversations, was thrilled to find himself crucial to the most significant scientific breakthrough, accompanied by the largest amount of cash he'd ever seen sitting in his new offshore bank account.

"Gentlemen, I am thrilled to unveil our new nanite program," Bernard announced, retrieving Le Silence 3 semi-automatic from a gleaming chrome case and shooting his newest assistant in the heart.

Teal's mind was busy with visions of lavish spending as he fell to the floor.

"What the fuck is this!" yelled a general as chaos erupted, voices raised in disbelief. "Ladies and gentlemen, don't panic," chuckled Bernard nervously as he placed his gun gently on the table and raised his hands to chest height, "why should we put our death in the hands of others?"

Amidst the stunned silence bouncing around the four walls, all eyes stared at Bernard, so no one noticed a discreet two-man team attaching electrodes to Teal's lifeless body.

"But before you accuse me of unnecessary mess-making, you might want to consult with him," Bernard gestured towards Teal.

All eyes shift to the body on the floor, realising he's no longer dead, his vitals displayed on the big glass screen, impossible to miss, and that was the point. Silence persisted, disrupted only by the clatter of china as a petite redhead entered with refreshments.

"Tea, anyone?" said Bernard nonchalantly as the redhead manoeuvred around the table, not even raising an eyebrow over the apparent shooting that had just taken place. "Someone must have briefed her," he mused as his audience's attention was riveted to the screen, as Teal began to mumble.

No one dared move as the reality of what they had witnessed sank in. Calmly, Bernard takes his seat at the head of the table, accepting a tea from the redhead as she seamlessly navigates the room.

"I understand this may be startling, but there is nothing so final as death to fully realise the cost of losing personnel, who are often carrying vital information essential to your operations but a fear of losing them means you often do not risk sending them on the very missions that require their involvement, but as you see from today that will no longer be a concern."

"What the fuck man!!" exclaims Teal as he raises a hand to his nearly healed bullet wound.

"Mr. Jackson will answer questions in about five minutes. Shall we discuss price?" Said Bernard, looking into the blood-drained faces of his captive audience.

"Gentlemen, welcome to the end of death…"

Mr. Andreas Finch

Friday 6th August

Surrounded by darkness, except for the glow of his desk lamp, Andy Finch commanded the space as he pressed 'print', quietly summoning 60 small brown bugs to emerge from his 3D printer.

Studying his reflection on the monitor, he pondered the recent growth of his dark blonde hair, unsure of its appeal. Asking his mum for her opinion was out of the question, as she was always biased when it came to him and his looks. He tilted his head from side to side, contemplating his features. He had always thought his nose was a bit long and maybe too flat, but

he had definitely inherited his mother's strong jawline and full lips. Still, he couldn't tell if he was good-looking or not.
He had received no complaints so far, which was a relief, and his reputation commanded respect, which he appreciated.

The printer finished with a ping, pulling his focus back to the final stages of his latest invention. The fine detail is exquisite in its precision, he thought, checking each bug under a magnifying glass. Each one was slightly different from the last.

He never tired of 3D printing; its applications were only limited by the owner's imagination, an aspect he exploited to the fullest. He loved technology. While he could use the computer to check and finish his work, Andy relished the tactile sensation of hands-on completion. As he deftly inserted tiny SIM cards into each bug, excitement fuelled his meticulous effort.

Thirty minutes later, with their command codes activated, the bugs came alive, scurrying within a box on his desk. Checking the monitor, he marvelled at their unique perspectives, each bug sending and receiving a slightly different view of his workstation.

Testing one, he flew her around the room in manual mode before switching to automatic. She manoeuvred through the shelving units with dexterity, avoiding all the obstacles he had placed in her path; her flight was agile and precise.

It's time to see if she'll keep all my secrets, he thought, placing a cup of water on his coffee table before breaking one of her wings.

She flew straight toward the cup and dove in. A fizzing sound followed, and water exploded out of the cup all over his coffee table, confirming the effectiveness of his insurance policy.

"Success!" he cried as his mum, Gloria, entered the basement with a tray of food. She was the pillar of his life—Gloria Finch, a well-groomed, curvy Italian blonde with a smart mouth, bull headed and confident. He owed her his life and loved her unconditionally. "Andreas, darling," she said in her soft Italian accent, stepping off his basement stairs,

"I noticed you haven't eaten recently."

This was a line that nearly all Italian sons heard whenever they were home for more than five minutes. Her concern for his neglected meals was a familiar routine.

"Oh yeah, I forgot," he replied, smiling as the smell of Bolognese sauce wafted across his desk.

"But I'm hungry now." He carefully set down a bug.

"Oh, please tell me those are just prints," she said, her eyes resting on the tray of crawling bugs.

"Ah yes, my Stegobiumpaniceum coming to a food counter near you… soon," he jested as he dug into his meal.

"That's not funny," she said, smoothing down the sides of her apron.

"Would you like a closer look?" he asked, offering her the whole box of bugs.

"No, and I don't want you flying those things around upstairs when we have another family gathering either."

"You said you wanted Aunty Fey to leave," he snickered between bites of spaghetti as she headed back up the basement stairs.

"Yes, but I didn't want her to die of a heart attack before she was out the front door," she added, waving her arms around as a tiny smile spread across her face.

"Thanks for the food; it's delicious."

"Why don't you ask your friend Swan over for dinner? I'll organize the food; all you will have to do is heat and serve."

Alum Rock is a television series set in 1985 and follows Abdul and Rahim, two young doctors from Pakistan who just arrived in Alum Rock, Birmingham. Their goal is to study for and take the PLAB (Professional and Linguistic Assessments Board) exam so they can practise medicine in the UK.

During the series, Abdul and Rahim come into conflict with each other and the local community whilst also facing their own internal struggles over a series of social, cultural and religious clashes.

While they are studying, they become tenants of Mr Khan who is living with his beautiful young wife Gul.

The following extract is taken from the end of the series where Rahim has arrived at an important conclusion.

Alum Rock by Aisha Noor

INT. KHAN'S HOUSE - DAY

The house is jam-packed with guests who have all brought food or audio cassettes in small envelopes for Rahim to be delivered when he gets back.

FATIMA an elderly neighbour is sitting in the living room beside Abdu, Rahim and Kahn.

Gul is serving tea to the guests while hiding half of her face with her shawl.

              FATIMA
Rahim is returning to Pakistan which leaves us sad but congratulations to Abdul, our new GP at Alum Rock.

Nazia enters with a tray full of biryani.

              NAZIA
The food is ready in the kitchen.

Some guests start to leave the living room for the kitchen.

              FATIMA

And congratulations to Abdul also for being engaged to Nazia.

                    ABDUL
Today is a day that brings contrasting emotions, much like life itself.
NASREN a young girl from the area turns back from the kitchen.

                   NASREN
A doctor marrying a nurse—how lucky!

                    KHAN
Do you know something, sister Fatima?

                   FATIMA
No, Khan, what is it I must know?

                    KHAN
         (Twirling his moustache)
I had the honour of asking for Nazia's hand from her parents, for my son Abdul!

The crowd cheers.

BUBLOO a young child is playing with Rahim's sleeve and pulling at his watch.

                   BUBLOO
Rahim Bhai when will you be back?

RANI a young woman who is a friend of the family stands and presents Abdul with a strange looking garland.

RANI
For Abdul. All the girls of Alum Rock made a garland of not very fresh flowers, just like you, stolen from the corner graveyard. You remember you used to present us with those stolen flowers; now we present them to you on this auspicious occasion of your job and wedding.

Again, the crowd cheers and laughs, while Abdul accepts the garland.

FATIMA
Rahim, son, why are you so quiet. You chose to return to Pakistan; do you regret it?

Rahim looks up, Gul is still pouring tea with her face half hidden but her eyes are red and tears are rolling down. She whips around, wiping off her tears,

RAHIM
No, Khala, I am not regretting my decision… I have responsibilities… my old parents need me, my sister needs to be married off… and anyway as an eye specialist, I may like to cure poor patients without fees.

ABDUL
Your salary will be basic, and instead of establishing a private evening practice

to top up your income, listen to him.
He's doing charity work—is that logical??
Not to me.

                FATIMA
Abdul, son, don't you have the same
responsibilities as your friend?

                ABDUL
Oh yes, I do, but you see. If I may earn
good money, my parents will afford a
luxurious life, maids, servants, a
gardener, a chef and a big house in a
plush locality. They won't miss me then.

                NAZIA
We are buying a new house too.

Everyone claps, congratulating.

                RANI
Where in Alum Rock are you buying this
house?

                NAZIA
Oh, no, not in Alum Rock anymore.
No, no do not get me wrong, we love Alum
Rock. Its… just we want to move out… just
for a bit of fresh air.

                BUBLOO
Rahim Bhai, when will you return? I want
to be a doctor like you.

Rahim kisses him on his cheek but says nothing. He seems lost for words and emotions.

POLLY, the parrot comes flying into the room. All look at her as she sits on Rahim's shoulder.

              POLLY
          I love you!

Everyone finds it amusing, and they clap. Rahim looks up. Covering her face Gul is watching.

Rahim holds Polly in his hands and kisses her. She nestles on his lap.

Printed in Dunstable, United Kingdom